The #MeToo Movement

Peggy J. Parks

ReferencePoint
Press®

San Diego, CA

© 2020 ReferencePoint Press, Inc.
Printed in the United States

For more information, contact:
ReferencePoint Press, Inc.
PO Box 27779
San Diego, CA 92198
www.ReferencePointPress.com

LIBRARY OF CONGRESS CATALOGING-IN-PUBLICATION DATA

Names: Parks, Peggy J., 1951– author.
Title: The #MeToo Movement/by Peggy J. Parks.
Description: San Diego, CA: ReferencePoint Press, Inc., 2020. | Includes
  bibliographical references and index. | Audience: Grades 10–12.
Identifiers: LCCN 2019035159 (print) | LCCN 2019035160 (ebook) | ISBN
  9781682827611 (library binding) | ISBN 9781682827628 (ebook)
Subjects: LCSH: Sexual abuse victims–Juvenile literature. | Sexual
  harassment—Juvenile literature. | Sex crimes—Prevention—Juvenile
  literature.
Classification: LCC HV6626 .P3654 2020 (print) | LCC HV6626 (ebook) | DDC
  362.88/3—dc23
LC record available at https://lccn.loc.gov/2019035159
LC ebook record available at https://lccn.loc.gov/2019035160

Contents

Silent No More

Society has long been plagued by a serious problem, but people have rarely talked about it. The problem is sexual harassment, in which someone verbally or physically harasses another individual in a sexual manner. This may happen in a variety of ways, such as when a supervisor makes sexually suggestive remarks toward an employee, either at work or a different location. Another example is someone in the workplace making unwelcome sexual advances toward a coworker or repeatedly making sexual jokes that demean people. An example of physical sexual harassment is when, without permission, an individual is touched, fondled, grabbed, pinched, or rubbed in a sexual manner. In short, says the Equal Employment Opportunity Commission, sexual harassment is any sexual-related behavior that affects someone's employment, interferes with people's work performance, or creates an "intimidating, hostile, or offensive work environment."[1]

In 2017 actress Ashley Judd spoke with the *New York Times* about being sexually harassed by film producer Harvey Weinstein. Investigative reporters Jodi Kantor and Megan Twohey were writing a story about sexual misconduct allegations against Weinstein that involved dozens of women and spanned nearly three decades. Judd, who had known Weinstein for years and starred in some of his movies, was asked to share any experience she may have had with his improper behavior. After a great deal of soul-searching, she agreed to be interviewed—and what she revealed helped bring down one of the most powerful men in Hollywood and played a major role in fueling a movement known as #MeToo.

The Whisper Network

Judd's first encounter with Weinstein was in 1997, when she was a young, up-and-coming actress. He invited her to a breakfast meeting at a hotel in Beverly Hills, California. When she arrived, she was told to meet him in his suite rather than in the restaurant, which she thought was a little odd. As soon as Weinstein opened the door—wearing his bathrobe—it was clear to Judd that his intentions were not to discuss her acting career. After refusing his offers of a massage and shoulder rub, and his request that she watch him take a shower, Judd knew she had to get out of there. "I said no, a lot of ways, a lot of times, and he always came back at me with some new ask," she says. "It was all this bargaining, this coercive bargaining."[2]

Although Judd did not discuss the incident publicly at the time, she had many private conversations with other actresses and individuals working in the film industry. In the process she learned that Weinstein's inappropriate behavior was common knowledge among women in Hollywood, who discussed it secretively with each other on what they called the "whisper network." For twenty years Judd remained secretive about Weinstein. Then in 2017, when approached by Kantor and Twohey, she decided it was time to open up about what he had done. Judd has since become an outspoken #MeToo advocate who encourages women to speak out about sexual harassment, rather than remaining silent. "We need to formalize the whisper network. . . . All those voices can be amplified," she says. "That's my advice to women. That and if something feels wrong, it is wrong."[3]

"If something feels wrong, it is wrong."[3]

—Ashley Judd, an actress and advocate for the #MeToo movement

In 2017 actress Ashley Judd spoke with the New York Times about being sexually harassed by film producer Harvey Weinstein. Judd has since become an outspoken #MeToo advocate.

A Pervasive Problem

Sexual harassment is not a new phenomenon, but neither has it been well studied. For the longest time, discussions of sexual harassment centered more on anecdotal evidence than actual research. But #MeToo helped change that, serving as a catalyst for more groups to start collecting information. One of these, Stop Street Harassment, launched an online survey in January 2018. The survey, which involved more than two thousand adults aged eighteen and older, found that sexual harassment and sexual assault pose a significant problem, especially for females. Of females who responded, 81 percent said they had been sexually harassed or assaulted at some point during their lives. The same was true of 43 percent of males. Verbal harassment was the most common, followed by unwanted touching in a sexual way.

Stop Street Harassment was also involved in a more recent (April 2019) survey on sexual harassment, and the prevalence was identical to that of 2018: 81 percent of women and 43 percent of men had experienced some form of sexual harassment and/or assault in their lives. Again, the most common type reported was verbal harassment, but a troubling number of people also faced other forms, such as being sexually touched or groped, physically followed, and/or flashed. "This report demonstrates that sexual harassment is prevalent and ubiquitous in the U.S., no matter who you are or where you live,"[4] says Anita Raj, director of the Center on Gender Equity and Health, which cosponsored the survey.

> "Sexual harassment is prevalent and ubiquitous in the U.S., no matter who you are or where you live."[4]
>
> —Anita Raj, director of the Center on Gender Equity and Health

Why Did They Not Report It?

Such research is crucial for gathering accurate data because most people do not report incidents of sexual harassment. This was one of the findings of a December 2018 study by researchers from the University of Massachusetts at Amherst's Center for Employment Equity. The researchers found that about 5 million employees are sexually harassed at work every year, and an astounding 99.8 percent never file formal charges. When people hear such statistics, a common question is, why would anyone keep such incidents to themselves?

Those who have been sexually harassed have their own reasons for staying silent, with the fear of losing their jobs the most common. Men (and sometimes women) who sexually harass others tend to be in positions of power, which gives them some level of control over their victims. "Sexual harassment is really not about sex," says James Campbell Quick, a professor of leadership and management at the University of Texas at Arlington. "It's about power and aggression and manipulation. It's an abuse of power problem."[5] An example of this is Weinstein, who got away with improper behavior for decades because of his power and prestige in the film industry. The fear that he would ruin young actresses' chance to succeed in movies kept revelations about his behavior confined to the whisper network for years.

Along with the fear of losing their jobs, the likelihood of co-worker retaliation often stops people from reporting sexual harassment. They may have seen their colleagues become hostile and turn against people who reported such incidents, and they may fear the same thing will happen to them. If so, they reason, their situation would be worse than if they had just kept quiet—which means it would not be worth the risk. "Many victims would rather stay silent and suffer through in the short term than face the consequences that speaking up could bring,"[6] says Kristina Udice, a New York City writer who specializes in gender equality and diversity issues.

Only the Beginning

As awareness of sexual harassment grows, people who have been the target of it may feel more comfortable speaking up. Encouraging people to do that—and ending society's tendency to blame the victim rather than the perpetrator—is at the heart of the #MeToo movement. Judd sometimes recalls her state of mind in 2017 when she decided to go public about Weinstein, and she finds what happened after that to be truly amazing. "We've just flung the barn doors wide open and the horses have run out," she says. "And the joy of the stampede has surprised me. I didn't know that it would be so joyous."[7]

Chapter ONE

A Hashtag Sparks a Movement

People typically assume that the #MeToo movement began in 2017 in the aftermath of the Harvey Weinstein scandal. But the movement was actually founded more than a decade earlier. It was the brainchild of Tarana Burke, a civil rights activist and social justice advocate from New York City. In 2006, while living and working in Selma, Alabama, Burke and her colleagues became aware of a disturbing number of girls and women of color who had been victims of sexual abuse and violence. These females needed help and support, as well as a safe place to talk about what happened without being afraid or ashamed.

At the time, social media was relatively new, and the social networking platform MySpace was just becoming popular. To increase the visibility of her work with sexual abuse victims, and to offer a virtual platform where they could communicate and support each other, Burke started a MySpace page titled *Me Too*—and was astounded at the response. "There was no such thing as viral back then. But if there was this would be as close to that as possible," says Burke.

> Within like a week or so, we had so many responses from women who were like, "Thank you for doing this," "This is really amazing," "How can we be involved," "We need help." And we realized this is bigger than we thought.[8]

Burke had no way of knowing that the movement she started would eventually become a massive global platform for change.

The Famous Milano Tweet

The "me too" message was well known to Burke's colleagues and people throughout the country who were familiar with her work. It was not widely known beyond those circles—until 2017, when the phrase "me too" was propelled into the spotlight by actress and activist Alyssa Milano. On October 15, 2017, Milano was angry and disgusted after reading articles about the many women who said Weinstein had sexually harassed or assaulted them. That night, while getting ready to go to bed, she received a text message from an acquaintance who attached a screenshot saying, "Suggested by a friend: if all the women who have been sexually harassed or assaulted wrote 'me too' as a status, we might give people a sense of the magnitude of the problem."[9]

> "I looked down at my daughter, sent the tweet, and went to sleep not knowing it was going to snowball."[10]
>
> —Actress and activist Alyssa Milano, on her original "me too" tweet

Milano had been sexually assaulted twice, once when she was a teenager, and she felt compelled to do as the screenshot suggested. She decided to tweet it to her followers. "I thought, you know what? This is an amazing way to get some idea of the magnitude of how big this problem is. It was also a way to get the focus off these horrible men and to put the focus back on the victims and survivors." To personalize the message, Milano added one sentence: "If you've been sexually harassed or assaulted, write 'me too' as a reply to this tweet," and then she sent it. "That was basically it," she says. "I looked down at my daughter, sent the tweet, and went to sleep not knowing it was going to snowball."[10]

And snowball it did. The next morning, when Milano checked her Twitter feed, there were at least fifty-five thousand replies marked with "me too." Most of the respondents had turned it into a hashtag, #MeToo, which quickly became the number one trending hashtag on Twitter—and it had spread far beyond the United States. In a 2018 article in *Foreign Affairs*, Pardis Mahdavi, who is acting dean of the Josef Korbel School of International Studies in Denver, Colorado, writes, "#MeToo took hold in every corner of the world. By the end of the day [on October 16, 2017], there were similar movements in multiple languages, including Arabic, Farsi, French, Hindi, and Spanish. Today, women in eighty-five different countries are using the hashtag to bring attention to the violence and harassment they face in daily life and to demand change."[11]

Milano later said that the overwhelming response to her tweet did not really surprise her; she had long been convinced that sexual harassment was a massive problem. What she was not expecting, though, was a different kind of response—tweets from women of color who were familiar with Burke and her work. They made it clear that the "me too" message had been around for more than a decade and it was Burke who deserved credit for starting the movement. Burke was initially also concerned.

Tarana Burke is credited with starting the #MeToo movement in 2006 when she created a MySpace page titled "Me Too," for victims of sexual abuse.

She had devoted her entire career to fighting sexual harassment and abuse among young black women. She was afraid that all her work would be buried under the avalanche of publicity that seemed focused on actresses and other famous white women. As Burke said in a 2018 interview: "I woke up to find out that the hashtag #metoo had gone viral and I didn't see any of the work I laid out over the previous decade attached to it. I thought for sure I would be erased from a thing I worked so hard to build."[12] As soon as Milano realized what had happened, she reached out to Burke by tweeting an apology. The two women began working together to promote the #MeToo movement.

A Heartbreaking Recollection

For years Tarana Burke has worked as an advocate for young women of color who have been sexually harassed or assaulted. But when she thinks about her first encounter with a young girl who turned to her for help, the memory is extremely painful. It occurred in the late 1990s, when Burke was working at a youth camp in Selma, Alabama. During a bonding session, several girls shared intimate stories about their lives. As she had done many times before, Burke listened to the girls and offered comfort as needed. The next day a thirteen-year-old girl named Heaven, who had been in the session, asked to speak with Burke privately. Burke writes:

> For the next several minutes this child, Heaven, struggled to tell me about her "stepdaddy" or rather her mother's boyfriend who was doing all sorts of monstrous things to her developing body. . . . I was horrified by her words, the emotions welling inside of me ran the gamut, and I listened until I literally could not take it anymore. . . . Right in the middle of her sharing her pain with me, I cut her off and immediately directed her to another female counselor who could "help her better." I will never forget the look on her face. I will never forget the look because I think about her all of the time. . . . I watched her put her mask back on and go back into the world like she was all alone and I couldn't even bring myself to whisper . . . me too.

Tarana Burke, "The Inception," JustBe Inc., 2013. https://justbeinc.wixsite.com/justbeinc/the -me-too-movement-cmml.

The Women Who Said "Me Too"

The responses to Milano's "me too" tweet came from all kinds of people, including many celebrities. Superstar Lady Gaga, who had been open about her own trauma as a rape survivor, was among the first celebrities to tweet a response. A number of actresses also responded, including Gabrielle Union, Anna Paquin, Patricia Arquette, Viola Davis, Deborah Messing, Rosario Dawson, and Evan Rachel Wood. Singer/songwriter Kimya Dawson tweeted "me too," as did comedian Lane Moore and former Fox News anchor Gretchen Carlson. Most women who tweeted #MeToo messages were not famous, however. As journalist Mary Pflum writes in an NBC News story, "Many women who were not household names also spoke out: nurses, teachers, engineers, florists, waitresses and students—mothers and daughters, sisters and wives."[13]

"A stranger tweeted back to me to stay strong."[15]

—Stephanie Angstadt, a seventeen-year-old girl who responded to the "me too" tweet

One young woman who responded was seventeen-year-old Stephanie Angstadt. When she saw Milano's "me too" tweet, she was living in a group home in Mississippi and says she was feeling "very cut off from the world."[14] Angstadt had been placed in protective custody after reporting that her father had sexually abused her from the time she was fifteen. On October 15, 2017, while looking at her Twitter feed, she saw tweet after tweet after tweet from women who were responding to Milano with their own "me too" messages. Seeing so many others who had been sexually harassed or assaulted made Angstadt realize she was not alone, and it gave her the courage to tweet about her own trauma. Immediately, people replied with messages of support. "A stranger tweeted back to me to stay strong,"[15] she says.

Nora Yolles Young, a hypnotherapist from Carrboro, North Carolina, also responded to Milano's "me too" tweet. While Young was in her twenties, she was on an archaeological dig with a group of students from the University of Redlands in California. One night, she says, a male student got drunk and sexually assaulted her. She reported what happened to her professor, who brushed her off. He told her, "Don't act like you didn't know what you were doing." Shocked, Young replied, "It sounds like you're saying I got what I asked for when this person tried to rape me." The professor did not deny her implication; instead, he merely said, "Boys will be boys."[16] Even though that incident occurred more than twenty years ago, Milano's tweet reminded Young of what happened, and she decided to speak up and say, "me too."

In 2017 actress Alyssa Milano, seen here at a rally in 2018, tweeted about sexual harassment and received a positive response. She eventually teamed up with Tarana Burke to promote the #MeToo movement.

Breaking the Silence

Because of the extraordinary courage it took for women to speak up about painful experiences, *Time* magazine selected a group of them to be profiled in its December 2017 Person of the Year issue. Contrary to the title, the issue did not focus on just one person. Rather, "The Silence Breakers," as it was titled, was a collective focus on women who were brave enough to share their personal stories with others. *Time* editor in chief Edward Felsenthal writes, "For giving voice to open secrets, for moving whisper networks onto social networks, for pushing us all to stop accepting the unacceptable, the Silence Breakers are the 2017 Person of the Year."[17]

Just as women of all walks of life responded to the #MeToo invitation, the same was true of those who were featured in "The Silence Breakers." A few famous women were profiled, including Milano, Ashley Judd, and singer/songwriter Taylor Swift. Burke was featured, as were a state senator, an engineer, a hospital worker, a corporate lobbyist, a hotel housekeeper, and a woman whose job is picking strawberries. The hospital worker, who remained anonymous out of concern for her family's safety, was sexually harassed by an executive at the hospital. She says the man repeatedly came on to her, and as is typical of sexual harassment victims, she questioned what she had done to provoke him. In the *Time* article, she remarked, "I thought, *What just happened? Why didn't I react?* I kept thinking, *Did I do something, did I say something, did I look a certain way to make him think that was O.K.?*"[18] The woman knows that having such thoughts is useless, as well as poisonous to the mind, but she has no idea how to stop them. She remembers the exact shirt she was wearing on one of the days, and she can still feel what it was like to have the man's hands on her body.

Swift was included in the article because of how she fought back after being sexually harassed in Denver, Colorado. On June 2, 2013, she was scheduled to perform at the Pepsi Center in Denver. Before the performance, she participated in a backstage meet and greet, which involved posing for photos with fans. While posing for a photo with Denver radio personality David Mueller, Swift felt him put his hand up the back of her skirt, grab her butt, and squeeze. "I squirmed and lurched sideways to get away from him," she says, "but he wouldn't let go." Swift was shocked and sickened by the incident, and she knew it had to be reported. "I figured that if he would be brazen enough to assault me under these risky circumstances and high stakes, imagine what he might do to a vulnerable, young artist if given the chance."[19] Her security staff notified Mueller's employer about the incident, and he was fired. Mueller, in turn, swore he was innocent and in 2015 sued Swift for $3 million in damages. She countersued for a symbolic $1, intending to send the message that women should be able to report sexual harassment and assault without fear of retaliation.

> "You should not be blamed for . . . the outcome of what happens to a person after he or she makes the choice to sexually harass or assault you."[20]
>
> —Singer/songwriter Taylor Swift

The trial took place two years later and lasted a week. Mueller's attorney badgered Swift with questions, accusing her of lying and asking if she felt guilty for causing Mueller to lose his job. She stood up to the lawyer, making it clear that he was not going to blame her for what his client did. At the close of the trial, the jury ruled in Swift's favor. She later spoke about the ordeal in an interview and acknowledged that blaming the victim is common:

> You could be blamed for the fact that it happened, for reporting it and blamed for how you reacted. You might be made to feel like you're overreacting, because society has made this stuff seem so casual. My advice is that you not blame yourself and do not accept the blame others will try to place on you. You should not be blamed for . . . the outcome of what happens to a person after he or she makes the choice to sexually harass or assault you.[20]

Pop star Taylor Swift was featured in a Time magazine cover story about the #MeToo movement. She recounted how she was sexually harassed backstage after one of her concerts in 2013.

#GirlsToo

People of all ages are affected by sexual harassment, but much of the #MeToo publicity has focused on adults. As a way of reaching out to teens with the #MeToo message, an organization called Girls Inc. started the #GirlsToo movement. The need for this is huge. According to the National Sexual Violence Resource Center, one in four girls is sexually assaulted by age eighteen, and two out of three girls are sexually harassed before that age. One of those girls is fifteen-year-old Savannah Thompson. During her entire three years of middle school, says Thompson, she was sexually harassed by one male student in particular, and sometimes his friends joined in. They called her names like "slut" and

Although females are sexually harassed at double or triple the rates of males, surveys have shown that males are also the targets of sexual harassment. One man who has spoken out is actor and singer Javier Muñoz, who is best known for playing the title role in the wildly successful Broadway musical *Hamilton*. On October 15, 2017, in response to Alyssa Milano's now-famous tweet, Muñoz wrote, "Me too. I don't know if [it] means anything coming from a gay man but it's happened. Multiple times."

Many people responded to Muñoz's tweet, including both women and men. They assured him that what he wrote indeed meant something, and that being male did not discount what he had experienced. They also praised him for having the courage to speak up.

Javier Muñoz (@JMunozActor), "Me too. I don't know if [it] means anything coming from a gay man but it's happened. Multiple times," Twitter, October 15, 2017. https://twitter.com.

"whore," and they grabbed her butt and developing breasts. She says teachers saw this happen and did nothing to stop it. "I got really bad anxiety from being sexually harassed," says Thompson. "I was scared to walk down the hallway or go to class and learn because I knew certain people would be there. I was really, really, extremely depressed and got to the place where . . . I felt really abandoned and alone."[21]

According to psychologist Christia Spears Brown, anxiety and depression are common among girls who have been sexually harassed. Also common among these girls are eating disorders, post-traumatic stress disorder, suicidal thoughts, and decreased academic motivation. Girls who are sexually harassed before age eighteen have an especially high risk of developing these and other problems. For that reason, says Brown, movements like #GirlsToo are sorely needed. Thompson, who now volunteers with #GirlsToo,

"I got really bad anxiety from being sexually harassed. I was scared to walk down the hallway or go to class and learn because I knew certain people would be there."[21]

—Savannah Thompson, a teenage sexual harassment survivor and #GirlsToo volunteer

18

says the movement is immersing young girls in the conversation about sexual harassment and is "allowing us the space and the resources to share our voices and our experiences."[22]

From Collective Pain to Collective Power

Since 2006, when Burke created a MySpace page called "Me Too," the movement she envisioned and founded has grown into a worldwide campaign against sexual harassment and sexual assault.

Burke, Milano, and others who have been outspoken advocates for the #MeToo movement say the effects have been powerful and profound. On the one-year anniversary of #MeToo, Milano shared her thoughts: "The most beautiful thing from all of this is not only women standing up and using their voices but standing up for each other in solidarity. The collective pain we've felt has turned into a collective power. It's amazing."[23]

Chapter TWO

Downfall of the Rich and Powerful

Before the #MeToo movement was catapulted into the public spotlight, women who reported sexual harassment incidents were rarely believed. This was especially true in cases in which there were no witnesses. When it was "her word against his," his denial of wrongdoing was typically considered more credible and believable than her accusations. But with the advent of #MeToo, that trend began to change. A large number of wealthy, powerful men were accused of sexual harassment—and unlike in the past, the women were not assumed to be lying or mistaken. Noreen Farrell, executive director of Equal Rights Advocates, explains, "Because of sheer number of the similarities of stories, we're actually exploring why it happened and not whether it happened. This feels different."[24]

The Weinstein Effect

Former media mogul Harvey Weinstein was the first of the rich and powerful men to be brought down as a result of the #MeToo movement. More than eighty women publicly accused Weinstein of sexual misconduct, with incidents ranging from verbal sexual harassment to rape. Many (although not all) of his accusers were famous actresses, including Ashley Judd, Rose McGowan, Asia Argento, Angelia Jolie, Gwyneth Paltrow, Uma Thurman, Salma Hayek, Kate Beckinsale, and Mira Sorvino. When these women began coming forward, one after another, to share their stories, Weinstein's insistent denials of wrongdoing grew weaker and weaker.

On October 8, 2017, Weinstein was fired by the Weinstein Company, the movie and television studio he co-founded. Also, after being pressured by members of the company's board of directors, he resigned from his post on the board. Later that same month, Weinstein was expelled from the Academy of Motion Picture Arts and Sciences. Referring to the academy's action as "an unprecedented public rebuke of a prominent industry figure," *Los Angeles Times* journalist Josh Rottenberg wrote, "The move marked the latest blow in Weinstein's stunning downfall and, in symbolic terms, amounts to a virtual expulsion from Hollywood itself."[25]

"Because of sheer number of the similarities of stories, we're actually exploring why it happened and not whether it happened."[24]

—Noreen Farrell, executive director of Equal Rights Advocates

#

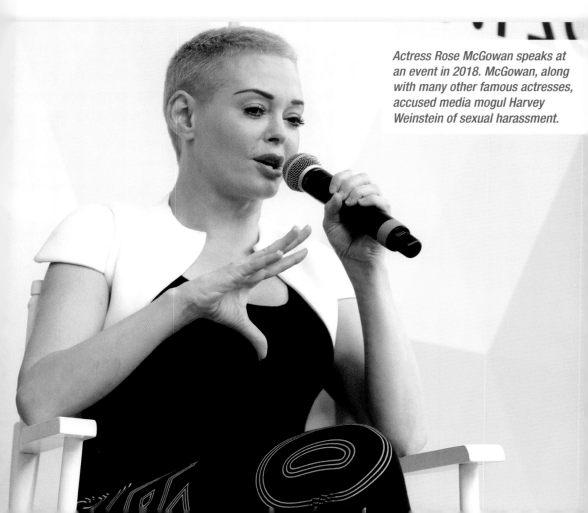

Actress Rose McGowan speaks at an event in 2018. McGowan, along with many other famous actresses, accused media mogul Harvey Weinstein of sexual harassment.

Weinstein's fall in the wake of dozens of publicly aired sexual misconduct allegations is not an isolated event. Other women have since come forward to accuse powerful men in various fields of similar conduct—and these men have lost their positions and reputations too. This phenomenon has been dubbed the Weinstein Effect, as entertainment journalist Elena Nicolaou explains: "The Weinstein Effect is the culture of silence that protects powerful men being rapidly eroded. Its survivors feeling emboldened to speak up against misconduct. And it's resulted in reports of workplace harassment skyrocketing." Were it not

A Dramatic Shift

The large number of powerful men who have been taken down by the #MeToo movement is a sign that sexual harassment is being viewed more seriously than ever before. Attorney, law professor, and women's rights expert Catharine A. MacKinnon refers to the large number of sexual harassment claims against these men as an "unprecedented wave of speaking out," and she refers to #MeToo as "the world's first mass movement against sexual abuse." In a March 2019 *Atlantic* article, MacKinnon writes:

> Until #MeToo, perpetrators could reasonably count on their denials being credited and their accusers being devalued to shield their actions. Many survivors realistically judged reporting to be pointless or worse, predictably producing retaliation. Complaints were routinely passed off with some version of "She isn't credible" or "She wanted it" or "It was trivial." A social burden of proof effectively presumed that if anything sexual happened, the woman involved desired it and probably telegraphed wanting it. She was legally and socially required to prove the contrary. . . . After four decades—or thousands of years, depending on when you start counting—the pervasive silence that walled off reports of sexual abuse crumbled. What was previously ignored or attributed to lying, deranged, or venial discontents and whiners began to be treated as disgraceful and outrageous misconduct that no self-respecting entity, including companies or schools, could accept being associated with.

Catharine A. MacKinnon, "Where #MeToo Came from, and Where It's Going," *Atlantic*, March 24, 2019. www.theatlantic.com.

for #MeToo's exposure of sexual harassment and sexual assault as serious, widespread, and pervasive, the silence would likely have continued. As Nicolaou writes, "In the past, these men may have been able to shoo away accusations through large settlements, or carefully worded public apologies—yet those deflections aren't protecting people any longer. Employers seem to be—gasp!—taking allegations seriously."[26]

Louis C.K.

Between October 2017, when the initial *New York Times* story about Weinstein was published, and April 2019, more than 250 men in positions of prestige and power had been publicly accused of some form of sexual misconduct. They represent a variety of industries, including film and television, music, the media, politics, financial services, law, science, and higher education, among others. One entertainer whose career was destroyed after sexual harassment accusations were made against him is comedian Louis Székely, better known by his stage name, Louis C.K. In November 2017 the *New York Times* ran a story about five women who shared startlingly similar accounts of his inappropriate sexual behavior. Upon hearing about these accounts, he surprised many people by admitting that the women's accusations were true. In a public statement, the comedian said:

> I learned yesterday the extent to which I left these women who admired me feeling badly about themselves and cautious around other men who would never have put them in that position. . . . I didn't think that I was doing any of that because my position allowed me not to think about it. There is nothing about this that I forgive myself for. And I have to reconcile it with who I am. Which is nothing compared to the task I left them with.[27]

Soon after the allegations became public and Székely confirmed their truth, his career began to crumble. On November 10,

Comedian Louis C.K., pictured at the 2012 Emmy Awards, was accused of sexual harassment by several women in 2017. Soon after the allegations became public, his career began to crumble.

2017, his publicist, Lewis Kay, cut ties with him, tweeting, "As of today, I no longer represent Louis C.K."[28] The comedian was also dropped by his management company, 3 Arts Entertainment, and HBO announced that he would not be doing his scheduled appearance on the network's *Night of Too Many Stars* fund-raiser. That same week Netflix announced that it would not go forward with a scheduled comedy special starring Louis C.K., and the television network FX announced that after eight years of working with the comedian, it was dropping him and his production company.

Matt Lauer

November 2017 was also a very bad month for popular news anchor Matt Lauer, who had cohosted NBC's *Today* morning show for twenty years. On November 29, 2017, Andy Lack, chair of NBC News, announced that Lauer had been fired. Lack stated:

> We received a detailed complaint from a colleague about inappropriate sexual behavior in the workplace by Matt Lauer. It represented, after serious review, a clear violation of our company's standards. As a result, we've decided to terminate his employment. While it is the first complaint about his behavior in the over twenty years he's been at NBC News, we were also presented with reason to believe this may not have been an isolated incident.[29]

The "detailed complaint," as referenced by Lack, was an account by a female NBC employee who accused Lauer of inappropriate sexual conduct. This began, the woman explained, in February 2014 while she and Lauer were stationed in Sochi, Russia, during the Winter Olympics, and it continued for several months afterward. The details of her complaint were not made public.

After Lauer's firing, a number of other women at NBC spoke up, saying that his inappropriate behavior was well known at the network. During a two-month investigation by the entertainment industry publication *Variety*, dozens of current and former NBC employees were interviewed. They described Lauer as being fixated on women's bodies and said he often made lewd comments verbally as well as by text message. He was said to freely ask about female coworker's sex lives and did not hesitate to name the female cohosts he would most like to sleep with. It was also widely known that Lauer had a button under his desk that allowed him to lock his office door without getting up from his chair. Such devices are not uncommon among top executives whose positions make privacy a must. In Lauer's

> "We received a detailed complaint from a colleague about inappropriate sexual behavior in the workplace by Matt Lauer. It represented, after serious review, a clear violation of our company's standards."[29]
>
> —Andy Lack, chair of NBC News

Actor and comedian Jeremy Piven is one of the men who lost a coveted acting job as a direct result of sexual harassment accusations against him. Piven is best known as the star of the HBO comedy series *Entourage*, in which he played an abrasive, ruthless, foul-mouthed womanizer named Ari Gold. When multiple women came forward to accuse him of sexual misconduct, Piven vehemently denied the accusations. He said all the women were lying, and that people believed the claims because he was being confused with his despicable TV character.

The claims against Piven ranged from physical aggression and groping to attempted rape. One of his accusers, who has remained anonymous, met Piven in the 1990s while he was in Montreal, Canada, filming the movie *Dr. Jekyll and Ms. Hyde*. She says he tried to force himself on her and she was able to fight him off and get away. "I guess he thinks he's this actor and he can do whatever the hell he wants to people," she says. "As a woman . . . you deal with this kind of thing all the time. But this was a little more violent than the other things that have happened to me. To have somebody force themselves on you like that—it made me feel very uncomfortable and grossed out." Based on the multiple sexual harassment allegations, in November 2017 TV network CBS announced that it was canceling Piven's series *Wisdom of the Crowd*. After losing his acting job, Piven started doing stand-up comedy in clubs.

Quoted in Krystie Lee Yandoli, "Exclusive: Three More Women Are Accusing Jeremy Piven of Sexual Misconduct," BuzzFeed News, January 27, 2018. www.buzzfeednews.com.

case, however, women saw the button in a different way, as a November 2017 *Variety* article explains: "It allowed him to welcome female employees and initiate inappropriate contact while knowing nobody could walk in on him, according to two women who were sexually harassed by Lauer."[30]

Because of the sexual harassment claims that led to Lauer's firing, his reputation was badly damaged. His wife left him and later filed for divorce. In 2019, when NBC produced a video to celebrate the *Today* show's twenty-fifth anniversary, Lauer was not invited to take part. And that same year, when a rumor circulatied that he was being considered for a morning anchor position at CNN, some employees of that network protested. This led to CNN chief Jeff Zucker making a public statement to denounce the rumor and emphasize that Lauer was not joining CNN. According to one employee, who wishes to remain anonymous, many at CNN considered that a welcome announcement. "The internal talk about Matt was that—if it turned out to be true—some senior female employees would refuse to work with him. There was palpable relief in the office after Jeff confirmed Matt isn't happening."[31]

Al Franken

When the #MeToo furor was building in the fall of 2017, men in a wide range of careers were being accused of sexual harassment, including some who held political office. Within a year, nine members of the US Congress had either resigned or declined to run for reelection after sexual misconduct claims were made against them. One was Al Franken, a Democratic US senator from Minnesota since 2009. Franken was accused of sexual harassment by multiple women, the first of whom was conservative radio host Leeann Tweeden.

On November 16, 2017, Tweeden posted a photo on her station's website that was taken in December 2006. Following a United Service Organizations (USO) trip to the Middle East to entertain troops stationed there, she and Franken, along with some others, were traveling home on a military plane. Tweeden recalls being exhausted and says she fell asleep soon after boarding the plane. In the photo, Franken is leaning over her as she sleeps, grinning at the camera, with his open hands hovering close to her breasts as though he was about to grab them. Tweeden did not see the photo until she was back in the United States and was reviewing all the photos from the trip. When she saw it, she was very upset, as she explains: "I couldn't believe it. . . . I felt violated. . . . Embarrassed. Belittled. Humiliated." Tweeden chose not to report the incident out of fear that it would hurt her professionally. "Even as angry as I was, I was worried about the potential backlash and damage going public might have on my career as a broadcaster."[32]

> "I felt violated. . . . Embarrassed. Belittled. Humiliated."[32]
>
> —Leeann Tweeden, a radio host who accused former US senator Al Franken of sexual harassment

Tweeden says she decided to speak out after hearing the stories of sexual harassment prompted by the #MeToo movement.

Following her accusations, as well as accusations by several other women, Franken's fellow Democratic senators were faced with a tough choice. They had talked among themselves about what they should do, and at first they resisted the notion of asking him to resign. But after the sixth complaint, they called for Franken's resignation. Although he denied sexually harassing Tweeden or any other woman, he resigned the following day.

Later, some who had known Franken for a long time questioned Tweeden's allegations, including two women who had gone on USO tours with him. Another development was a change of heart by some of his fellow senators, who said that asking him

Al Franken, a Democratic senator from Minnesota, was accused of sexual harassment by multiple women in 2017. Although he denied sexually harassing any of the women, he eventually resigned.

to resign was a mistake and they regretted it. One of them was Heidi Heitkamp, a former senator from North Dakota, who told a *New Yorker* reporter, "If there's one decision I've made that I would take back, it's the decision to call for his resignation. It was made in the heat of the moment."[33] Franken himself says that he deeply regrets resigning from his position as a US senator, but at the time he felt like he had no other choice.

Ken Friedman

Another man whose career was derailed because of sexual harassment allegations is restaurateur Ken Friedman, who is famous in New York City for his wildly popular West Village restaurant the Spotted Pig. Friedman was the subject of a December 12, 2017, story in the *New York Times* titled "Ken Friedman, Power Restaurateur, Is Accused of Sexual Harassment." *New York Times* investigative journalists conducted more than two dozen interviews with former employees of the Spotted Pig and other restaurants owned by Friedman and his business partner, acclaimed chef April Bloomfield. The article states:

> Ten women said that Mr. Friedman, 56, had subjected them to unwanted sexual advances: groping them in public, demanding sex or making text requests for nude pictures or group sex. Many others also said that working for him required tolerating daily kisses and touches, pulling all-night shifts at private parties that included public sex and nudity, and enduring catcalls and gropes from guests who are Mr. Friedman's friends.[34]

One former employee who was quoted in the same article was Natalie Saibel, who had been a longtime server at the Spotted Pig. She told reporters that in 2015, when she and Friedman were in a dining room that was packed with restaurant patrons, he ran his hands over her buttocks and then her groin. He excused the groping by making a joke that he was searching her pockets to make sure she was not carrying a forbidden cell phone. Another former employee, Carla Rza Betts, was the wine director at the Spotted Pig and two other Friedman restaurants. She recalls one night in 2010 when Friedman took her to a rooftop bar ostensibly to scope out competitive establishments. Without asking, she says, he leaned over and planted a kiss on her lips. "In the moment, you are not thinking at all," she says. "He's your boss. You don't punch him. You just don't kiss back, and pull away and try to shake it off." She says that Friedman sent a series of suggestive texts afterward, which made her uncomfortable. Yet despite what had happened, Rza Betts continued working for him. "You hike up your bootstraps and you work," she says. "That's how we all survived working for him."[35] Finally, in 2013 Rza Betts decided she had had enough and quit her job.

On the same day the *New York Times* article about Friedman was published, his parent company announced that, effective immediately, he would be taking an indefinite leave of absence from managing his restaurants. Soon after that, Bloomfield announced that she was dissolving their business relationship. "It is over," she tweeted on December 13, 2017. "I pledge that in any workplace I am part of the employees will be judged by performance only. I pledge to show respect, always, and that under my watch no employee will endure this kind of pain again."[36] As of 2019 the Spotted Pig was still a successful restaurant, but its reputation had been badly tarnished—just as Friedman's had. He has been the subject of innumerable media reports, many of which refer to him as a "disgraced" restaurateur.

> "I pledge to show respect, always, and that under my watch no employee will endure this kind of pain again."[36]
>
> —April Bloomfield, on her decision to dissolve her business relationship with disgraced restaurateur Ken Friedman

A Reckoning

Although no two cases of sexual harassment are identical, a common thread ties them together: the alleged perpetrators are typically in positions of power, and by engaging in inappropriate sexual conduct, they are abusing that power. This was true of Harvey Weinstein, who could make or break the careers of aspiring actresses. It was true of Louis C.K., who was admired by the up-and-coming comedians he confessed he had sexually harassed. Matt Lauer was in a position of power as one of the most highly paid television hosts, and as a US senator, Al Franken held a great deal of power and prestige. And before he was disgraced, Ken Friedman was considered one of the preeminent restaurateurs in the United States. Whether these men are guilty of everything their accusers allege is something the public may never know. What is known, however, is that the sexual offenses of which they are accused cost them their careers and their reputations.

Chapter THREE

Women Make Political History

In a December 2018 *New York Times* article, journalist Maya Salam reflected on the year that was coming to a close. "It has been called the Year of the Woman," she said, "and rightly so—defined by historic political victories in the United States, #MeToo-fueled uprisings around the world, and women . . . who pushed fear aside to be heard." Indeed, the fourteen months between #MeToo's explosive resurgence on social media and the end of 2018 was a time of extraordinary change and political history making in the United States. As Salam wrote, "Women upended the political landscape."[37]

Salam's comment about politics was in reference to the November 6, 2018, midterm elections, which included hundreds of congressional, state, and local races. In those elections, more women were elected to public office than at any other time in US history. They were elected to both houses of Congress and to various state governmental positions.

The #MeToo Influence

Although many factors likely played a role in this extraordinary wave of female political victories, the #MeToo movement has been credited with being a strong catalyst. This became apparent in a February 2018 survey by the women's equality nonprofit Barbara Lee Family Foundation, which involved one thousand women and men who said they intended to vote in the 2018 midterms. An April 2018 summary of the survey states, "This new research . . . shows that the majority of voters take sexual harassment seriously; say that it will influence their voting decisions; and look more favorably upon candidates who take a strong stance against sexual harassment."[38]

During the survey, 51 percent of all respondents said they would never vote for a candidate who did not make addressing sexual harassment a priority. Among millennial women (those in their early twenties to late thirties), the percentage was the highest of all respondents: 65 percent would refuse to vote for someone who did not make addressing sexual harassment a priority. When asked about the current climate of sexual harassment, 30 percent of respondents said it made them more likely to vote for female candidates in general. Millennial women felt strongest about the issue, with 60 percent saying the current sexual harassment climate made them more likely to vote for women. When asked about voting for someone who had been accused of sexual harassment, 52 percent of all respondents—and 73 percent of millennial women—said they would never vote for such a person. The authors of the April 2018 summary write, "Sexual harassment is not a niche issue—it is one with the potential to make a real difference at the ballot box."[39]

Julie McClain Downey of the political action committee Emily's List says that throughout the 2018 campaign she saw a trend: women voters responding positively to female candidates who were willing to share their own #MeToo stories. For the first time, voters could see that the candidates running for office actually understood what sexual harassment felt like. And just as important, these candidates would not pretend that it does not exist. Downey explains, "Seeing all of this play out in a way where suddenly you realize that you're not alone, and you can use your voice and your vote to elect someone who will address these issues and not just sweep them under the rug, is pretty remarkable."[40]

Making History at the State Level

The 2018 elections were notable not just for the number of women who won public office but also for the large number who ran for office. This was especially evident in state races. According to the National Conference of State Legislatures (NCSL), more than thirty-five hundred female candidates ran for state legislative positions during the 2018 midterms. This represented a 28 percent increase over 2016. And a large percentage of the women who ran in 2018 won their elections. "When women run, they win," says the NCSL's Katie Ziegler. "So, what happens when more women run than ever before? They break all kinds of records."[41]

One woman who was victorious in her state was Anna Eskamani, who was elected to the Florida legislature with 57 percent of the vote. After her win was confirmed, she spoke about the events that influenced her decision to run for office. "This last year we saw an undeniable shift in how we tolerate sexual harassment and how we talk about it," she said. Eskamani says her initial inspiration to run for public office was the 2016 presidential election. Several other occurrences helped make up her mind, as she explains: "It was the Women's March in 2017 that further solidified my aspirations to do this work, and it was the #MeToo movement that reminded me that it's so important that we not only run but that we win."[42]

> "When women run, they win. So, what happens when more women run than ever before? They break all kinds of records."[41]
>
> —Katie Ziegler, program manager for the National Conference of State Legislatures Women's Legislative Network

Scores of other women also made huge strides in winning state government positions. Janet Mills, a Democrat from Maine, was one of them. When Mills was elected governor on November 6, 2018, she became the first female ever to hold that top office in her state. Kristi Noem, a Republican from South Dakota, was also elected governor, and she, too, was the first woman in her state to ever hold that office. Another state with a new female governor

New members of the US House of Representatives gather for a photo. In the 2018 midterm elections more women were elected to public office than at any other time in US history.

is Michigan, whose citizens elected Democrat Gretchen Whitmer, only the second woman in history to hold that post. Whitmer has spoken publicly about being raped while she was in college, and she is a strong supporter of the #MeToo movement. "I'm here to lend my voice to this movement and encourage others to do that," she said in a video posted on social media. "Because it's only by talking about the issues that we face every day that we can actually solve them."[43]

Texas elected a number of trailblazing females during the November 2018 election. According to the *Texas Tribune*, 40 percent of Texas women who ran for seats in the US Congress, as well as state judicial positions and other high-level state offices, won their races. The number of women in the Texas House of Representatives increased from twenty-nine to thirty-two. Women led the Democrats in flipping twelve seats in the state House from Republican to Democrat, which was the biggest shift since 2010. Texas League of Women Voters president Grace Chimene believes that a "new era of voter enthusiasm" will play a major role in women choosing to run for political office in the future. "It's the resurgence of interest in our democracy and interest within the new voters and young voters that's going to push women running for office,"[44] she says.

Beverly Powell is one of the newly elected Texas state senators. She agrees with the sentiment that 2018 was the year of the woman and says it is only the beginning—that women are "gaining their voice more and more every day." Powell predicts more political victories for women in the coming years. "We're going to see a number of women in the state Legislature and Congress increase," she says, "and that's a powerful tool to make sure that we can implement the kind of change in this nation that's important to families and all of our citizens."[45]

Women Elected to Federal Office

As in the state elections, an unprecedented number of women ran for seats in the US Congress in November 2018—and a large percentage of them won. Among the winners was Kyrsten

A Notable Milestone

For as long as the United States has existed, men have controlled the US Congress. Over the years, women have made inroads in winning political offices, but this has been a slow, arduous process. An important factor in people's voting decisions is typically whom they consider the most competent and qualified to serve. In the past, a widespread belief was that men were better suited emotionally to hold public office. That perspective still exists, but according to a major survey published in 2018, people who hold that view are now in the minority.

The General Social Survey (GSS) has been conducted in the United States since 1972, and its goal is to monitor societal change, including measuring people's views of gender and society. The 2018 GSS took place from April through November of that year and involved 2,348 American adults. When asked whether women are just as suited emotionally for politics as men, 85 percent of respondents said they were. This is a radical change in perspective compared to several decades ago. In 1974, for instance, only 49 percent of respondents said women were equally qualified to hold political office.

The four new congresswomen known as "the Squad" (pictured from left to right: Rashida Tlaib, Ilhan Omar, Alexandria Ocasio-Cortez, Ayanna Pressley) make a statement at a press conference in 2019. All four are women of color, and all are progressive Democrats.

Sinema, a Democrat from Tucson, who became the first Arizona woman to be elected to the US Senate. Texans Veronica Escobar and Sylvia Garcia won seats in the US House of Representatives and became the first Latinas to represent their state in Congress. Sharice Davids of Kansas and Deb Haaland from New Mexico also made history as the first two Native American women elected to Congress. And Kendra Horn, a Democrat from Oklahoma, scored an unlikely victory over incumbent Republican Steve Russell, a well-known war hero. In winning that election, Horn flipped a House seat that had been in Republican control for more than forty years. Also significant is that when Horn was elected, she became the first woman of the Democratic Party ever to represent Oklahoma in Congress.

Of all the women who started brand-new jobs in the House of Representatives in 2019, none have captured as much media attention as four congresswomen known as "the Squad." All four are women of color, and all are progressive Democrats. They have shown themselves to be outspoken and unafraid to voice their strong opinions in speeches, in interviews, and on social media. The group includes Ayanna Pressley from Boston, Massachusetts; Alexandria Ocasio-Cortez from New York City; Rashida Tlaib from Detroit, Michigan; and Ilhan Omar from Minneapolis, Minnesota. Their nickname came about soon after they were elected. On November 12, 2018, the women were in Washington, DC, and posing for a photo together. Ocasio-Cortez posted the photo to her Instagram account with the simple caption, "Squad." The photo quickly went viral, and from that day on, they were known as "the Squad."

"For generations men have dominated every power, every narrative. We're standing in our power and we're claiming our space, and it's about damn time."[46]

—Ayana Pressley, a US representative from Boston, Massachusetts

#

All four women are considered trailblazers for their own individual reasons. Pressley, who is African American, had to overcome many obstacles on the way to becoming a candidate and member of Congress. Her opponent, Michael Capuano, is white and had served in Congress for ten terms, or a total of twenty years. As a child Pressley was sexually abused, and at age nineteen, while attending Boston University, she was raped. As a result of that trauma, she has a special connection with the #MeToo movement. Pressley believes that her constituents are best represented by someone who has lived through hard times and understands the challenges they face day to day. And she views the record number of women elected to Congress as a positive, hopeful sign of much-needed change for the future. "For generations men have dominated every power, every narrative," Pressley says. "We're standing in our power and we're claiming our space, and it's about damn time."[46]

Ocasio-Cortez, who is often referred to as AOC, also overcame numerous obstacles on her path to the US House of Representatives. She won her election with 78 percent of the votes. At twenty-nine years old, she became the youngest woman ever to serve in Congress. "We made history tonight," Ocasio-Cortez said in a speech after her election. "This is what is possible when everyday people come together in the collective realization that all our actions, no matter how small or how large, are powerful, worthwhile and capable of lasting change."[47]

By winning her election in November 2018, Tlaib captured a congressional seat that was previously held by Democrat John Conyers, who was the longest-serving member of Congress. Conyers had resigned the previous year after being accused by multiple former aides of sexual harassment. Tlaib and Omar collectively made history, since they were the first two Muslim women ever to be elected to Congress.

When Omar won her House seat, she replaced Keith Ellison, a Democrat who had served in the House for twelve terms (twenty-four years). She is the first member of Congress to wear a hijab, the traditional head covering worn by many

Ilhan Omar is the first member of the US Congress to wear a hijab. She sought and was granted a religious exception for Congress's no-hats rule.

Muslim women. As soon as her term started in January 2019, Omar was reminded of Congress's no-hats rule, which applies to everyone who serves, whether male or female. She sought and was granted a religious exception to the rule, but she was still harshly criticized for wearing the hijab. One staunch critic was E.W. Jackson, a conservative pastor and lawyer who complained that because of her the House floor would look like an Islamic republic. Omar was quick to respond, tweeting: "Well sir, the floor of Congress is going to look like America. . . . And you're gonna have to just deal."[48]

Keeping the Momentum Going

There have been numerous signs that the #MeToo movement has made a positive difference for women in the United States, such as the number of female candidates elected to public

Power Shift

The #MeToo movement was a catalyst for some momentous changes in the United States—from a record number of female candidates elected to public office to massive increases in sexual harassment reporting. According to the *New York Times*, as of October 2018, more than two hundred wealthy, powerful men had been ousted from their jobs after being publicly accused of sexual harassment. This determination was based on an in-depth analysis by *New York Times* reporters. They found that in 2016, fewer than thirty high-profile men had resigned or been fired after being accused of sexual misconduct. After the Harvey Weinstein scandal in the fall of 2017, which caused #MeToo awareness to soar, that number climbed to more than two hundred. When their vacated positions were filled, 43 percent of the men were replaced by women. "We've never seen something like this before," says Joan Williams, a law professor who specializes in gender studies. "Women have always been seen as risky, because they might do something like have a baby. But men are now being seen as more risky hires."

Quoted in Audrey Carlson et al., "MeToo Brought Down 201 Powerful Men. Nearly Half of Their Replacements Are Women," *New York Times*, October 29, 2018. www.nytimes.com.

office. Even though women have been serving in political office for more than a century, state and federal legislative posts have been overwhelmingly held by men. While it would be idealistic to say that this trend will change anytime soon, there is every reason to believe that women are making headway and

that momentum will continue in the coming years. As Emily's List president Stephanie Schriock said after the November 2018 election, "History has been made and we're never going back."[49]

Unintended Consequences

Washington, DC, political consultant Katie Packer Beeson is an avid supporter of the #MeToo movement. She has experienced sexual harassment in her professional life, as have most of the women she knows. Largely because of the movement, these and other women have felt empowered to speak up about their experiences. "We started telling our stories, the media started paying attention and many men have been held accountable for these bad acts and paid heavy prices," says Beeson, "and rightfully so."[50] Yet despite her strong support for #MeToo, Beeson cannot help wondering if, in some instances, it has gone too far.

Presumed Guilty

Beeson is especially troubled by the prevailing view that any woman with a sexual harassment story is telling the truth and any man accused of sexual harassment is automatically seen as guilty. That seems grossly unfair to Beeson, as she writes: "Lately I have begun to wonder if this cultural shift has created a 'ready, fire, aim' mentality where we immediately believe every woman who comes forward with a claim and refuse to give the men any chance to tell their side of the story."[51]

Beeson observed this attitude when one of her friends lost his job after being accused of sexual harassment by a female subordinate. The woman said they had been involved in a sexual relationship and he had used that against her by refusing to give her a raise in pay or an opportunity for promotion. "He was fired," says Beeson, "no questions asked."[52]

Despite their friendship, Beeson asked the man some tough questions about what happened between him and the woman. He did not deny that they were sexually involved, but he said they were both willing partners in the relationship. He denied doing anything to hold the woman back in her career. In fact, he said it was she who had demanded a substantial raise, and when he refused, she was angry and likely sought revenge. Beeson writes:

> "Shouldn't we expect to provide evidence before we are able to destroy someone else's career and reputation?"[53]
>
> —Katie Packer Beeson, a political consultant in Washington, DC

> I can't help wondering if there has been a massive rush to judgment that may have destroyed his career, and his good name, while protecting her career and reputation. Should he have dated a subordinate? Probably not. Should the punishment be getting fired and characterized as some kind of sex predator? I don't think so. . . . Shouldn't we expect to provide evidence before we are able to destroy someone else's career and reputation? A story should not be enough, particularly in cases where there is no pattern of bad action.[53]

The Fear Factor

In the wake of the #MeToo movement, what Beeson's friend went through is a fear that many men share. Even those who detest sexism and sexual harassment worry about what might happen if they are accused of something they did not do. "Some men have voiced concerns to me that a false accusation is what they fear," says attorney Stephen Zweig, who is with the New York City law firm FordHarrison. "These men fear what they cannot control."[54]

Surveys have also shown that #MeToo has led to men being more uneasy around female coworkers. Whereas in the past men felt comfortable kidding around with female coworkers, they now wonder whether that sort of thing is taboo. If they touch the shoulder of a woman as a sign of support, will they be accused of sexual harassment? What if they tell an off-color joke or accidentally say something that a woman finds offensive? Could this lead to their being fired? These sorts of questions have bothered Steve Wyard, a veteran sales associate from Los Angeles. During a December 2017 interview with the Associated Press, Wyard spoke of his concerns. "Have we gotten to the point now where

In the wake of the #MeToo movement, some men say they are uneasy around female coworkers. Some worry that a supportive gesture such as a pat on the back could be misconstrued as sexual harassment.

men can't say, 'That's a nice dress' or 'Did you do something with your hair?'" asks Wyard. "The potential problem is you can't even feel safe saying, 'Good morning' anymore."[55]

Men are not alone in being concerned about these issues. During a series of focus groups in March 2018, women also expressed worry about the potential negative effects of #MeToo on men they care about. One woman spoke about her father, who encountered a troubling situation at his workplace. A female worker asked him for help moving a large box, and he said, "Yes, dear, I'll get that for you." The woman promptly told him never to call her "dear" again. "He was so upset when he got home," says his daughter. "He was like, 'I didn't mean anything by it.'"[56]

Another focus group participant, Shar'Ron Maxx Mahaffey, shared her fears about men being wrongfully accused of sexual harassment or assault. She is especially concerned for her son, as she explains: "I cannot imagine, with the level of respect he shows me and his sisters and my sisters, that he could ever do something like that. But what if someone just accused him of doing it? Am I just supposed to take her word for that, knowing who my son is?"[57]

In early 2019 social psychologist Pragya Agarwal had a conversation with a young man who worked as an investment banker in New York City. He told Agarwal that he had become very afraid of working with women and would not consider mentoring a woman. When she asked him why, he said he did not know how to act around women anymore, could not be sure of how his actions would be perceived, and was afraid of being accused of sexual harassment. "He had a whole lot of other reasons," says Agarwal. "But mainly that he had no incentive to mentor women. He would go through extra hassle for no rewards, and live with constant fear of being alone with them, of even looking at them in case that glance was perceived as lecherous, flirtatious, and inappropriate."[58]

> "Have we gotten to the point now where men can't say, 'That's a nice dress' or 'Did you do something with your hair?'"[55]
>
> —Steve Wyard, a sales associate from Los Angeles
>
> #

On October 8, 2018, US Navy veteran Pieter Hanson was taking a college exam when he was bombarded with text messages. Hanson hurried through the exam and then ran into the hallway to check his phone. In one text after another, friends warned him about a tweet posted by his mother that had gone viral. It had cast him as a supporter of #HimToo, a counter-movement that was founded to protest unproven (and often false) allegations of sexual harassment and assault. The tweet was accompanied by a photo of Hanson in his navy uniform and said, "This is MY son. He graduated #1 in boot camp. He was awarded the USO award. . . . He is a gentleman who respects women. He won't go on solo dates due to the current climate of false sexual accusations by radical feminists with an axe to grind. I VOTE. #HimToo."

Hanson was appalled to see the tweet—and the hundreds of angry responses. He had been an ally of #MeToo from the beginning, and he did not support the #HimToo backlash. "It doesn't represent me at all," he said to reporters. Hanson did not have a Twitter account, but he joined so he could set the record straight. On October 9, 2018, he wrote, "That was my Mom. Sometimes the people we love do things that hurt us without realizing it. Let's turn this around. I respect and #BelieveWomen. I never have and never will support #HimToo. I'm a proud Navy vet, Cat Dad and Ally."

Quoted in Meagan Flynn, "'This Is MY Son': Navy Vet Horrified as Mom's Tweet Miscasts Him as #HimToo Poster Boy—and Goes Viral," *Washington Post*, October 9, 2018. www.washington post.com.

Research Revelations

People's views about #MeToo—both positive and negative—have been captured in numerous surveys, such as one by NPR and Ipsos in October 2018. More than one thousand adults participated in the survey, with 40 percent saying they felt the movement had gone too far. Exactly what "too far" meant to these participants was not defined in the survey, but some shared their thoughts in follow-up conversations. The factors mentioned included a rush to judgment when someone has been accused, the prospect of unproven accusations ruining people's reputations and careers, and the chance of accusers claiming sexual misconduct when something much less serious actually took place. "We have females that come forward and make false allegations, jumping on the #MeToo bandwagon, and it's ruined a lot of guys' lives,"[59] says survey participant Nate Jurewicz.

Fears over being accused of sexual harassment have also caused many professional men to drastically limit interactions with female colleagues. This was one of the findings of a March 2019 survey by the women's support organization Lean In, which involved more than fifty-one hundred men and women. Of male managers surveyed, 60 percent said they were uncomfortable engaging in common workplace interactions with women, such as one-on-one meetings and mentoring—a 32 percent jump over a survey conducted the year before. More than one-third of male managers (34 percent) said they have actively taken steps to avoid having to interact with a female colleague outside of work, often because they were nervous about how it would look to

Some male managers report being uncomfortable engaging in common workplace interactions with women. Some say they try to avoid meeting with female colleagues.

other people. *Forbes* senior contributor Kim Elsesser writes, "It's not that men are afraid that they will inadvertently harass some-one like the men accused during the early days of #MeToo. . . . Instead, men are more worried about how it looks to meet alone with women or dine alone with women. They don't want to give any hint of impropriety."[60]

Strained Relationships, Diminished Opportunities

This sort of wariness has severely strained relationships between men and women in the workplace. According to New York City attorney John Singer, who has represented both men and women in sexual harassment cases, #MeToo has had a chilling effect on relationships between male and female coworkers. "Men are either scared to be alone with female colleagues or clients or more skittish about what to say,"[61] says Singer. He has heard from both male and female clients that women are being excluded from meetings and social outings. In addition to keeping women from moving up the career ladder, he says, that sort of isolation is making it harder for them to simply do their jobs, whether that involves meeting with clients or teaming up with men on sales calls.

> "Men are either scared to be alone with female colleagues or clients or more skittish about what to say."[61]
>
> —John Singer, an attorney from New York City

Research has shown that the field of law is one area where workplace relationships between men and women have become seriously strained. According to an October 2018 article in *American Lawyer*, many male attorneys are intentionally avoiding working closely with women, as one female attorney from New York City explains: "It's a genuine fear. I've talked to men—well-meaning ones—who say they're scared of being taken the wrong way by women, who don't know how they should interact with female associates and colleagues. I'm afraid this will mean men will exclude us even more from relationship-building opportunities."[62]

Because of #MeToo, some male executives have made it a rule to only socialize with men outside of work. This sort of shunning behavior in the workplace is hurting women and interfering with their professional growth.

The financial industry has also suffered from deteriorating relationships between male and female colleagues. In December 2018 Bloomberg News reported that on Wall Street, men were adopting controversial strategies for dealing with women at work. The report was based on interviews with more than thirty senior executives in finance who spoke of their uneasiness at being alone with female colleagues. One said that he will not meet with women in rooms without windows, and he also keeps his distance in elevators. Another established a new rule for himself: no business dinners with women aged thirty-five or younger. Other changes men spoke of included having after-work drinks only with men, never with women, and leaving the office door open even during private meetings with female coworkers.

This sort of shunning behavior in the workplace is hurting women and interfering with their professional growth. "Women are grasping for ideas on how to deal with it, because it is affecting our careers," says Karen Elinski, who is senior vice president at Wells Fargo & Company. "It's a real loss."[63]

Punished for Speaking Up

Along with harm to workplace relationships, another ominous by-product of the #MeToo movement is retaliation. After being silent for so long about sexual harassment, women felt empowered to speak up—and many lost their jobs because of it. According to the Equal Employment Opportunity Commission, which enforces civil rights laws and registers complaints, retali-

A Rejection of "#MeToo Fatigue"

In a January 2019 commentary published in the *Hill* political newspaper, National Organization for Women president Toni Van Pelt addressed the backlash against the #MeToo movement. Referring to it as "ferocious," Van Pelt sees it as a manufactured crisis that was intentionally created to divert attention from the real focus of the movement: that sexual harassment is a very real, pervasive problem. She writes:

> The same groups that have been undermining women's equality for so long are busy denying the epidemic of sexual violence and marginalizing survivors who come forward at great personal risk. It's even been suggested that "#MeToo fatigue" is settling in and that the movement is a phase that will soon pass by. That's not true.
>
> Women will not be silenced even as we face a disinformation and propaganda campaign engineered by a culture of men protecting other powerful men. The serious problem of sexual harassment and assault is being marginalized by those who would keep the focus on celebrity misconduct or business scandals, rather than dealing with the root of the problem: These defenders of privileged men who abuse women ignore the deep and lifelong economic and psychological impact that this discriminatory treatment has on women.
>
> Abusers must be removed from their positions of power and brought to justice, but we need to take the conversation about sexual violence past the "gotcha" phase and the prurient details of lewd acts and find concrete ways to end the culture of abuse.

Toni Van Pelt, "The Myth of #MeToo Fatigue," *Hill* (Washington, DC), January 3, 2019. https://thehill.com.

ation is a factor in about three-fourths of the sexual harassment charges filed, and it is becoming more common. "The number of retaliation charges has been climbing," says commission member Victoria Lipnic. She refers to retaliation as "the next frontier in terms of what we need to deal with on the harassment front."[64]

Journalist Diana Falzone has spoken with many women who faced retaliation after reporting sexual harassment to their employers. In early 2019, for instance, she got a phone call from a former television personality. The woman had sued a large corporation for sexual harassment and said she was now unable to find an on-camera job or even an agent who would represent her. The woman told Falzone:

> "The very same people who publicly applaud you for speaking up about bad behavior will never hire you into their own organizations because you are forever pegged as a whistleblower and a troublemaker."[65]
>
> —A former female television personality #

The very same people who publicly applaud you for speaking up about bad behavior will never hire you into their own organizations because you are forever pegged as a whistleblower and a troublemaker. On your deathbed, you will probably feel that you have done the moral thing by speaking up, but in the years you are alive, you are very cognizant of the toll your decision to come forward has taken on your life and your career path.[65]

Falzone emphasizes that there is no media black list. Yet numerous women, all of whom settled high-profile lawsuits against serial sexual harassers, have told her of their struggle to continue working in their careers after standing up for themselves. As branding and marketing expert Scott Pinske remarked to Falzone, "It would be awful if one of the unintended consequences of the 'Me Too' movement is that employers are now so paranoid of being sued, they're quietly blackballing the victims who had the strength and courage to stand up for themselves. I hope that's not the case, but common sense says otherwise."[66]

Uncertainties Abound

The #MeToo movement has made a positive difference in the lives of women throughout the world. Those who were sexually harassed or sexually assaulted finally knew they were not alone, they had nothing to be ashamed of, and they had every right to stand up for themselves. But along with that side of the movement have been some unintended consequences that are not so positive. Some men have lost their jobs and their reputations because of accusations that, for the most part, have not been aired in court or given a full and fair hearing of any sort. The fear of crossing a line of impropriety has many men avoiding interactions with women in the workplace, which puts a strain on relationships and limits women's ability to advance in their careers. These and other problems associated with #MeToo must be resolved, or the movement could be blamed for doing more harm than good.

Chapter FIVE

More Work to Be Done

In a September 25, 2018, *USA Today* editorial, Gretchen Carlson discusses the profound changes that have taken place because of the #MeToo movement. Carlson is a journalist and female empowerment advocate who was formerly with Fox News. After enduring years of sexual harassment by Fox chief executive officer Roger Ailes—much of which she captured on video with her iPhone—Carlson filed a sexual harassment lawsuit against him in July 2016. She writes, "There was no #MeToo hashtag then . . . and no real support system for women facing harassment and its aftermath." Carlson says that thanks to the #MeToo movement, the conversation about sexual harassment has shifted "180 degrees in terms of visibility and the recognition that abuse is everywhere."[67]

Still, the country has a long way to go before the problem of sexual harassment is solved. The reality is, fixing this generations-long blight on society is a massive endeavor that will take a great deal of time and effort. What is lacking, according to #MeToo advocates, is an expansive platform of policies and laws that are designed to fix the root problem—that sexual harassment remains pervasive, and those who are victims of it have few options to protect themselves and seek recourse. Carlson writes, "If #MeToo takes down a few powerful perpetrators without helping the vast majority of everyday working women, it will be a failure. Creating lasting change is the crucial next step."[68]

A #MeToo Champion

Carlson has spoken out a great deal about sexual harassment and has helped countless women who have experienced it themselves. One of her efforts was founding the Gretchen Carlson Leadership Initiative, an educational program that offers free workshops and legal services to women throughout the United States. Participants receive training in harassment and discrimination policies and may take advantage of resources to get free, much-needed legal help when they need it. "That's the number one thing that these women need," says Carlson, "to be able to bounce their story off of a legal expert and say, 'here's what happened to me. Do I have a case?' This is about, yes, feeling empowered at the end, but [also] being educated."[69]

Carlson is also a leader in the fight for legislation called the Ending Forced Arbitration of Sexual Harassment Act. When employees are forced into arbitration, they present their case in a closed-door meeting to an independent person known as an arbitrator. When employees are required to sign contracts with forced arbitration clauses, if they sue a perpetrator for sexual harassment, they are not allowed to take their cases before a judge or jury. #MeToo advocates reject this practice for reasons Carlson explains:

> It's a way to systematically keep women silent. . . . The workplace will say, "oh this is so advantageous for you because it's cheaper and we'll help you pick the arbitrator, and no one will ever have to know about it." You don't get the same amount of witnesses and you get no appeals. You might get a paltry settlement and then you never work in your profession ever again. And the perpetrator gets to stay on the job—so they get to not only continue working while you don't, they get to continue to harass, potentially. It's this massive cover up.[70]

In 2019 the arbitration bill was improved and the name was changed to the Forced Arbitration Injustice Repeal (FAIR) Act. In September of that year the US House of Representatives passed the bill with an overwhelming majority. Whether the Senate would also pass it was unknown as of October 2019. But if passed, the law would restore accesses to the courts to millions of American workers who were previously forced to sign arbitration agreements.

Slow Going in the Nation's Capital

As powerful as the #MeToo movement has proved to be, there has been very little legislative action in Congress. As Carol Moody, president of the women's advocacy group Legal Momentum, explains, "Everybody thinks some massive, massive change in laws has happened with the #MeToo movement. But it hasn't."[71] Under federal law, sexual harassment (a form of sex discrimination) violates the Civil Rights Act of 1964. But #MeToo advocates emphasize that existing laws are ineffective at protecting people from sexual harassment, and they stress the need for stronger legislation.

One law that Congress did pass in 2018 was called the Congressional Accountability Act. It strengthens a 1995 law that protects congressional staff members from being sexually harassed by lawmakers. This action was hailed as long overdue by people who are familiar with working conditions on Capitol Hill, where sexual harassment is known to be a serious, pervasive problem. In April 2018 more than thirteen hundred former congressional staff members signed a letter addressed to US Senate leaders, candidly describing the seriousness of the problem and sharing their own personal experiences. The letter described a climate of fear, a complicated and confusing process for reporting sexual harassment, and a system that was designed to protect members of Congress rather than the victims of sexual harassment. On December 21, 2018, President Donald Trump signed the Congressional Accountability Act into law. #MeToo advocates were encouraged by the legislation, as were members of Congress who sponsored it. In a statement released after the bill was passed, the sponsoring legislators wrote, "We believe this is a strong step towards creating a new standard in Congress that will set a positive example in our nation, but there is still more work to be done."[72]

Other anti–sexual harassment laws have also been proposed. For instance, Senators Kamala Harris (California), Jacky Rosen (Nevada), and Richard Blumenthal (Connecticut) introduced the Combating Sexual Harassment in Science Act in April 2019. The proposed law focuses on people working in the STEM fields. Careers in science, tech, engineering, and math are heavily male dominated, with females representing only about 25 percent of workers. Research has shown that sexual harassment is alarmingly common among people who work in STEM careers.

One study was conducted in 2018 by the National Academies of Sciences, Engineering, and Medicine. It found that women working in STEM careers endure the highest rate of sexual harassment of any fields outside the US military. The study also showed that about 90 percent of women in STEM careers who report sexual misconduct experience job-related retaliation. The gravity

Time's Up

In the fall of 2017, shortly after #MeToo went viral on social media, a group of women in the entertainment industry got together to create an action plan. These women—three hundred in all—were outraged about the rampant sexual harassment in their industry, and their anger incentivized them to do something. The group's website explains:

Time's Up was born out of the need to turn pain into action. . . . As we grappled with the reality that 80 to 90 percent of leadership in our industry was male . . . we realized systemic change was necessary. We broke into groups to work on addressing different issues, which led to working groups focusing on issues like safety, equity and power. . . . As we addressed our own industry, we also knew that we had the opportunity—and responsibility—to create change for women everywhere.

A major Time's Up accomplishment was creation of the Legal Defense Fund, which provides legal and financial support for women who have pursued sexual misconduct claims in the courts. Nearly eight hundred attorneys are involved with the fund, with many taking cases and charging reduced rates or no fees at all. It was launched on the GoFundMe platform and raised more than $22 million in just two months—the most successful GoFundMe campaign of all time. "Together, we are seizing this unprecedented moment and transforming it into meaningful and institutionalized change across culture, companies and laws," says the Time's Up website. "And we're just getting started."

Time's Up, "History," January 1, 2018. www.timesupnow.com.

of this problem is what prompted Harris, Rosen, and Blumenthal to propose the Combating Sexual Harassment in Science Act. It would authorize $17.4 million in federal funding to address the causes and consequences of sexual harassment in STEM work-places. "STEM fields already suffer from gender inequality," says Blumenthal. "We should be making it easier for women and other underrepresented groups to get into these industries, not turning a blind eye to the kind of unacceptable harassment and discrimi-nation that make it even harder for them."[73]

In 2019, US senator Kamala Harris (pictured) introduced an anti-sexual harassment law. The proposed law focuses on people working in the STEM fields.

State Legislative Action

State governments have accomplished much more than the federal government in addressing sexual harassment. A February 2019 publication by the National Conference of State Legislatures said that "an unprecedented amount of legislation on sexual harassment and sexual harassment policies"[74] had been passed during 2018. State laws addressed the expulsion of legislators who commit sexual harassment, criminalizing sexual harassment in state legislatures, and making harassment training mandatory for legislative staff.

One endeavor of the National Women's Law Center (NWLC) is called 20 States by 2020, in which state legislators commit to strengthening legal protections against sexual harassment and sexual violence by the year 2020. According to a July 2019 report by the NWLC, fifteen states had passed such laws, and this was a direct result of the #MeToo movement. "Momentum is building among

> "Momentum is building among both conservative and progressive state legislators to pass reforms to fight harassment and abuse in the workplace, and that's exciting to see."[75]
>
> —Emily Martin, vice president of the National Women's Law Center

both conservative and progressive state legislators to pass reforms and fight harassment and abuse in the workplace," says NWLC vice president Emily Martin, "and that's exciting to see. . . . This is a movement that's shifting workplace culture and the laws that shape it—and we are on the path to achieving real change in 20 states by 2020."[75] The NWLC report shows that ten states enacted key sexual harassment prevention measures that mandate training and policy requirements for employees. These include California, Connecticut, Delaware, Illinois, Louisiana, Maryland, New York, Oregon, Vermont, and Washington. Some states expanded workplace harassment protections for the first time to include independent contractors, interns, and graduate students.

In Maryland the Disclosing Sexual Harassment in the Workplace Act took effect on October 1, 2018. This law protects the right to file sexual harassment claims and to do so without fear of retaliation. Earlier that same year New York lawmakers approved legislation that requires all state contractors to have sexual harassment policies in place and to submit a declaration of those policies. Also, all public and private employers in the state must have sexual harassment policies in place and provide yearly training to all their workers.

In California, legislators passed several bills that were inspired by the #MeToo movement. In large part, legislative progress in the state came about because existing sexual harassment policies were not working. In October 2017 more than 140 women—including legislators, senior legislative aides, and lobbyists—signed an open letter to California lawmakers. The letter told of what they described as a pervasive culture of sexual harassment perpetrated by powerful men within the state legislature. The letter stated:

As women leaders in politics, in a state that postures itself as a leader in justice and equality, you might assume our experience has been different. It has not. Each of us has endured, or witnessed or worked with women who have experienced some form of dehumanizing behavior by men in power in our workplaces. Men have groped and touched us without our consent, made inappropriate comments about our bodies and our abilities. Why didn't we speak out? Sometimes out of fear. Sometimes out of shame. Often these men hold our professional fates in their hands.[76]

The letter sparked California state legislators into action. They held a series of public hearings and began working on a collection of new sexual harassment laws. One is Senate Bill 1343, which requires employers with five or more workers to provide sexual harassment training to employees and supervisors. This is a change from 2005, when a similar bill applied only to employers with fifty or more employees. Another new piece of legislation is the Legislative Employee Whistleblower Protection Act. This law makes it a criminal and civil offense for legislators (or certain leg-

Washington, DC, attorney Ally Coll has long been outspoken about sexual harassment issues. In the wake of #MeToo's explosive rise in awareness and support, Coll cofounded the Purple Campaign, a group that works to end workplace sexual harassment through stronger corporate policies and more effective laws. In 2019 she was approached by a woman who had been sexually harassed at her workplace and had just gone through the process of reporting it. The woman believed her experience could help others who were going through similar difficulties, and she asked Coll whether there were any groups that enabled women to support each other. "Her question made me realize the answer was no," says Coll. So, together with political consultant Anna Kain, she decided to create one.

The group's purpose is to provide women with a safe, supportive space to share their experiences with sexual harassment. "We realized . . . that there were a lot of people looking to connect with others to share these experiences and looking for support and resources and guidance on navigating them," says Coll, "and that there wasn't an existing structure or place or environment for them to meet with other people and to connect with others." Coll and Kain agree that it would be hard to imagine a group like theirs coming together if the #MeToo movement did not exist.

Quoted in Lissandra Villa, "Dozens of Women Have Accused Powerful Men in DC of Sexual Harassment. Now They're Creating a Space to Talk About It," BuzzFeed News, April 26, 2019. https://buzzfeed.com.

islative employees), to retaliate against a staff member who has reported a legal violation, including sexual harassment.

In addition, California lawmakers passed a bill that protects underage employees who work in entertainment. The law mandates that before an employer in the entertainment industry can receive a permit to hire a minor, the employees (aged fourteen to seventeen) and a parent must undergo training in sexual harassment prevention. They must also receive instructions on how to report such offenses should they occur.

Industry Efforts

While tougher laws are an important step in fighting sexual harassment, industry leaders must also be committed to it. It is important for them to take a hard look at their own policies and see what is working and what needs to be improved. This seems to be happening throughout the United States, as Joan Fife, a labor and employment attorney from San Francisco, explains:

> I'm sure that many people would have expected there to be more prompt legislation passed and signed into law on both the state and federal level. I think that companies have responded much more quickly. . . . Going forward voluntarily, without waiting for the law to change, that's how best practices are created.[77]

> "Going forward voluntarily, without waiting for the law to change, that's how best practices are created."[77]
>
> —Joan Fife, labor and employment attorney from San Francisco, California
>
> #

In 2019 the employee relations company HR Acuity released a special report called #MeToo in the Workplace. More than 150 organizations worldwide, representing 4 million employees, were surveyed about sexual harassment prevalence, policies, and procedures. The survey found that 69 percent of companies already had procedures in place for responding to sexual harassment complaints or were planning to develop these procedures in the near future. The report also noted that 72 percent of employees and 76 percent of managers had already received sexual harassment awareness training or would do so in the near future.

Several Silicon Valley tech giants have implemented policies intended to prevent sexual harassment and to better address complaints. In November 2018, for example, Google and Facebook announced that they were ending their policies of forcing workers to settle sexual harassment claims through private arbitration. Instead, employees will be allowed to pursue their claims in court. Microsoft also ended its forced arbitration policy—and actually did so a year before Google and Facebook. #MeToo advocates applauded these decisions, such as Angela Cornell, the director of the Cornell University School of Law Labor Law

In 2018, Google announced that they were ending their policies of forcing workers to settle sexual harassment claims through arbitration. Instead, employees will be allowed to pursue their claims in court.

Clinic. "It's just one minuscule part of one statute, but do I think it's positive? I absolutely think it is," says Cornell. "I can't see how enforcement of sexual harassment can be done effectively with mandatory arbitration language in place."[78]

Looking Back, Moving Forward

The #MeToo movement has proved to be a powerful catalyst in the fight against sexual harassment. Not much has been done at the federal government level, but motivated legislators continue to advocate for meaningful change. State government progress has varied, with some states taking little or no action, and a few taking more aggressive steps to pass new laws. Many industry leaders are showing their commitment to end sexual harassment by surveying employees, implementing new training programs, and streamlining policies for reporting and addressing sexual harassment complaints. Those who are most passionate about #MeToo feel that not enough has been done about the problem of sexual harassment, and that may be true. But in a relatively short time, incredible progress has been made. As Carlson writes, "Our culture has fundamentally changed."[79]

Introduction: Silent No More

1. Equal Employment Opportunity Commission, "Facts About Sexual Harassment." www.eeoc.gov.
2. Quoted in Jodi Kantor and Megan Twohey, "Harvey Weinstein Paid Off Sexual Harassment Accusers for Decades," *New York Times*, October 5, 2017. www.nytimes.com.
3. Quoted in Stephanie Zacharek et al., "The Silence Breakers," *Time*, December 6, 2017. https://time.com.
4. Holly Kearl and Joseph Diebold, "New Study Shows High Prevalence of Sexual Harassment and Assault, and Much of the Public Believes Survivors," UCSD Center on Gender Equity, April 30, 2019. www.stopstreetharassment.org.
5. Quoted in Brendan L. Smith, "What It Really Takes to Stop Sexual Harassment," *Monitor on Psychology*, American Psychological Association, February 2018. www.apa.org.
6. Kristina Udice, "It's Not Just Harvey Weinstein: Why Sexual Harassment in the Workplace Goes Unreported," FairyGodBoss, 2018. https://fairygodboss.com.
7. Quoted in Jasmyn Belcher Morris and Emma Bowman, "Actress Ashley Judd's #MeToo Moment Was Driven by a 'Commitment' to Her Younger Self," NPR, March 2, 2018. www.npr.org.

Chapter One: A Hashtag Sparks a Movement

8. Quoted in Chris Snyder and Linette Lopez, "Tarana Burke on Why She Created the #MeToo Movement—and Where It's Headed," Business Insider, December 13, 2017. www.businessinsider.com.
9. Quoted in Nadja Sayej, "Alyssa Milano on the #MeToo Movement: 'We're Not Going to Stand for It Any More,'" *Guardian* (Manchester), December 1, 2017. www.theguardian.com.
10. Quoted in Sayej, "Alyssa Milano on the #MeToo Movement."
11. Pardis Mahdavi, "How #MeToo Became a Global Movement," *Foreign Affairs*, March 6, 2018. www.foreignaffairs.com.

12. Quoted in Paulina Cachero, "19 Million #MeToo Tweets Later: Alyssa Milano and Tarana Burke Reflect on the Year After #MeToo," *Makers* (blog), October 15, 2018. www.makers.com.
13. Mary Pflum, "A Year Ago, Alyssa Milano Started a Conversation About #MeToo. These Women Replied," NBC News, October 15, 2018. www.nbcnews.com.
14. Quoted in Pflum, "A Year Ago, Alyssa Milano Started a Conversation About #MeToo."
15. Quoted in Pflum, "A Year Ago, Alyssa Milano Started a Conversation About #MeToo."
16. Quoted in Pflum, "A Year Ago, Alyssa Milano Started a Conversation About #MeToo."
17. Edward Felsenthal, "The Choice," *Time*, December 6, 2017. https://time.com.
18. Quoted in Zacharek et al., "The Silence Breakers."
19. Quoted in Eliana Dockterman, "'I Was Angry.' Taylor Swift on What Powered Her Sexual Assault Testimony," *Time*, December 6, 2017. https://time.com.
20. Quoted in Dockterman, "'I Was Angry.'"
21. Quoted in Ayanna Runcie, "#MeToo for Youth: #GirlsToo Focuses on Teens' Sexual Trauma," CBS News, April 2, 2019. www.cbsnews.com.
22. Quoted in Runcie, "#MeToo for Youth."
23. Quoted in Pflum, "A Year Ago, Alyssa Milano Started a Conversation About #MeToo."

Chapter Two: Downfall of the Rich and Powerful
24. Quoted in Elena Nicolaou, "The Weinstein Effect, Explained," Refinery29, November 15, 2017. www.refinery29.com.
25. Josh Rottenberg, "Harvey Weinstein Expelled from Motion Picture Academy," *Los Angeles Times*, October 14, 2017. www.latimes.com.
26. Nicolaou, "The Weinstein Effect, Explained."
27. Louis C.K., "These Stories Are True," *New York Times*, November 10, 2017. www.nytimes.com.
28. Lewis Kay (@lewiskay), "As of today, I no longer represent Louis C.K.," Twitter, November 10, 2017, 4:49 p.m. https://twitter.com.

29. Andy Lack, "Transcript: 'Today' Anchor Matt Lauer Fired by NBC News," NBC News, November 29, 2017. www.nbcnews.com.
30. Quoted in Ramin Setoodeh and Elizabeth Wagmeister, "Matt Lauer Accused of Sexual Harassment by Multiple Women," *Variety*, November 29, 2017. https://variety.com.
31. Quoted in Emily Smith, "Jeff Zucker Denies Rumors Matt Lauer Will Be Joining CNN," Page Six, May 8, 2019. https://pagesix.com.
32. Leeann Tweeden, "Senator Al Franken Kissed and Groped Me Without My Consent, and There's Nothing Funny About It," KABC, November 16, 2017. www.kabc.com.
33. Quoted in Jane Mayer, "The Case of Al Franken," *New Yorker*, July 22, 2019. www.newyorker.com.
34. Julia Moskin and Kim Severson, "Ken Friedman, Power Restaurateur, Is Accused of Sexual Harassment," *New York Times*, December 12, 2017. www.nytimes.com.
35. Quoted in Moskin and Severson, "Ken Friedman, Power Restaurateur, Is Accused of Sexual Harassment."
36. Quoted in Hillary Dixler Canavan, "April Bloomfield on Ken Friedman: 'I Know That It Wasn't Enough,'" Eater, December 13, 2017. www.eater.com.

Chapter Three: Women Make Political History

37. Maya Salam, "2018: Year of the Woman, in 5 Powerful Quotes," *New York Times*, December 28, 2018. www.nytimes.com.
38. Barbara Lee Family Foundation, "New Research: Voters, Candidates, and #MeToo," April 2018. www.barbaraleefoundation.org.
39. Barbara Lee Family Foundation, "New Research."
40. Quoted in Emily Shugerman, "The #MeToo Movement Takes Office After Winning Elections Across the U.S.," Daily Beast, November 7, 2018. www.thedailybeast.com.
41. Katie Ziegler, "Election 2018: Women Ran, Women Won," *NCSL State Legislatures Magazine*, November/December 2018. www.ncsl.org.

42. Quoted in Ally Boguhn, "The 'Personal Is Political' for Women Running for Office in the #MeToo Era," Rewire, July 24, 2018. https://rewire.news.

43. Quoted in Shugerman, "The #MeToo Movement Takes Office After Winning Elections Across the U.S."

44. Quoted in Marissa Evans, "2018 Was the Year of the Woman in Texas. Candidates Say It's 'Not a One-Time Deal,'" Texas Tribune, November 8, 2018. www.texastribune.org.

45. Quoted in Evans, "2018 Was the Year of the Woman in Texas."

46. Quoted in Kayla Epstein, "For Ayanna Pressley, the Beauty of Unexpected Wins Led to Congress and a Historic Office," Washington Post, January 16, 2019. www.washingtonpost .com.

47. Quoted in Carla Herreria, "Alexandria Ocasio-Cortez Proclaims 'We Made History' in Electrifying Victory Speech," Huffington Post, November 7, 2018. www.huffpost.com.

48. Ilhan Omar (@IlhanMN), "Well sir, the floor of Congress is going to look like America. . . And you're gonna have to just deal," Twitter, December 6, 2018, 12:07 a.m. https://twitter .com.

49. Quoted in Lauren Gambino, "'Truly the Year of the Woman': Female Candidates Win in Record Numbers," Guardian (Manchester), November 7, 2018. www.theguardian.com.

Chapter Four: Unintended Consequences

50. Katie Packer Beeson, "Has #MeToo Gone Too Far?," U.S. News & World Report, February 12, 2018. www.usnews.com.

51. Beeson, "Has #MeToo Gone Too Far?"

52. Beeson, "Has #MeToo Gone Too Far?"

53. Beeson, "Has #MeToo Gone Too Far?"

54. Quoted in Gillian Tan and Katia Porzecanski, "Wall Street Rule for the #MeToo Era: Avoid Women at All Cost," Bloomberg, December 3, 2018. www.bloomberg.com.

55. Quoted in John Rogers, "In Wake of Harassment Cases, Men Wonder If Hugging Women Is Still OK," Houston Chronicle, December 8, 2017. www.chron.com.

56. Quoted in Anna North, "Why Women Are Worried About #MeToo," Vox, April 5, 2018. www.vox.com.

57. Quoted in North, "Why Women Are Worried About #MeToo."
58. Pragya Agarwal, "In the Era of #MeToo Are Men Scared of Mentoring Women?," *Forbes*, February 18, 2019. www .forbes.com.
59. Quoted in Tovia Smith, "A Year Later, Americans Are Deeply Divided over the #MeToo Movement," NPR, October 31, 2018. www.npr.org.
60. Kim Elsesser, "60% of Male Managers Are Uncomfortable in Job-Related Activities with Women—Here's Why," *Forbes*, May 17, 2019. www.forbes.com.
61. Quoted in Emily Peck, "MeToo Backlash Is Getting Worse," Huffington Post, May 17, 2017. www.huffpost.com.
62. Quoted in Meghan Tribe, "The #MeToo Backlash Is Building," *American Lawyer*, October 26, 2018. www.law.com.
63. Quoted in Tan and Porzecanski, "Wall Street Rule for the #MeToo Era."
64. Quoted in Alex Press, "Women Are Filing More Harassment Claims in the #MeToo Era. They're Also Facing More Retaliation," Vox, May 9, 2019. www.vox.com.
65. Quoted in Diana Falzone, "'You Will Lose Everything': Inside the Media's #MeToo Blacklist," *Vanity Fair*, April 16, 2019. www.vanityfair.com.
66. Quoted in Falzone, "'You Will Lose Everything."

Chapter Five: More Work to Be Done

67. Gretchen Carlson, "To Succeed, #MeToo Must Target America's Laws, Not Just a Few Powerful Men," *USA Today*, September 25, 2018. www.usatoday.com.
68. Carlson, "To Succeed, #MeToo Must Target America's Laws, Not Just a Few Powerful Men."
69. Quoted in Liz Cantrell, "Gretchen Carlson Is on a Mission to Help Women Who Have Been Sexually Harassed," *Town & Country*, May 10, 2019. www.townandcountrymag.com.
70. Quoted in Cantrell, "Gretchen Carlson Is on a Mission to Help Women Who Have Been Sexually Harassed."
71. Quoted in Cara Kelly and Aaron Hegarty, "#MeToo Was a Culture Shock. But Changing Laws Will Take More than a Year," *USA Today*, October 4, 2018. www.usatoday.com.

72. Quoted in Jennifer Bendery, "Congress Is Finally Dealing with Its MeToo Problem," *Huffington Post*, December 12, 2018. www.huffpost.com.
73. Quoted in MeriTalk, "Senators' Bill Would Curb Sexual Harassment in STEM Fields," April 5, 2019. www.meritalk.com.
74. Selena Saucedo, "2018 Legislation on Sexual Harassment," National Conference of State Legislatures, February 11, 2019. www.ncsl.org.
75. Quoted in National Women's Law Center, "Fifteen States Have Passed New Laws Protecting Workers from Sexual Harassment in Wake of #MeToo, NWLC Report Reveals," National Women's Law Center, July 25, 2019. https://nwlc.org.
76. Quoted in Adam Nagourney and Jennifer Medina, "Women Denounce Harassment in California's Capital," *New York Times*, October 17, 2017. www.nytimes.com.
77. Quoted in Charisse Jones, "#MeToo One Year Later: Cosby, Moonves Fall, Sex Harassment Fight at Work Far from Over," *USA Today*, October 4, 2018. www.usatoday.com.
78. Quoted in Jena McGregor, "Analysis: Google and Facebook Ended Forced Arbitration for Sexual Harassment Claims. Why More Companies Could Follow," *Washington Post*, November 12, 2018. https://www.washingtonpost.com.
79. Carlson, "To Succeed, #MeToo Must Target America's Laws, Not Just a Few Powerful Men."

Books

Gretchen Carlson, *Be Fierce*. New York: Center Street, 2017.

Jim DeRogatis, *Soulless: The Case Against R. Kelly*. New York: Abrams, 2020.

Laurie Collier Hillstrom, *#MeToo Movement*. Santa Barbara, CA: ABC-CLIO, 2019.

Linda Hirshman, *Reckoning: The Epic Battle Against Sexual Abuse and Harassment*. Boston: Houghton Mifflin Harcourt, 2019.

Heather C. Hudak, *#MeToo Movement*. New York: Crabtree, 2019.

Jodi Kantor and Megan Twohey, *She Said: Breaking the Sexual Harassment Story That Helped Ignite a Movement*. New York: Penguin, 2019.

Mirande Valbrune, *#MeToo: A Practical Guide to Navigating Today's Cultural Workplace Revolution*. Miami: Employee Relate, 2018.

Internet Sources

Nanette Asimov, "#MeToo Movement Spurs #HimToo Backlash: 'People Don't Want to Believe,'" *San Francisco Chronicle*, October 13, 2018. www.sfchronicle.com.

Tarana Burke, "#MeToo Was Started for Black and Brown Women and Girls. They're Still Being Ignored," *Washington Post*, November 9, 2017. www.washingtonpost.com.

Alix Langone, "#MeToo and Time's Up Founders Explain the Difference Between the 2 Movements—and How They're Alike," *Time*, March 22, 2018. https://time.com.

Wendy Lu, "What #MeToo Means to Teenagers," *New York Times*, April 19, 2018. www.nytimes.com.

Catharine MacKinnon, "Where #MeToo Came from and Where It's Going," *Atlantic*, March 2019. www.theatlantic.com.

Ayanna Runcie, "#MeToo for Youth: #GirlsToo Focuses on Teens' Sexual Trauma," CBS News, April 2, 2019. www.cbsnews.com.

Nancy Jo Sales, "MeToo in School: Too Many Children Are Sexually Harassed by Classmates," Teen Kids News, September 20, 2018. https://teenkidsnews.com.

Nadia Sayej, "Alyssa Milano on the #MeToo Movement: 'We're Not Going to Stand for It Anymore," *Guardian* (Manchester), December 1, 2017. www.theguardian.com.

Joanne N. Smith, "#MeToo Isn't Just for Adults," *Essence*, May 7, 2019. www.essence.com.

Kelly Wallace, "Will #MeToo Be a Turning Point for Younger Girls Too?," CNN, January 1, 2018. www.cnn.com.

Stephanie Zacharek et al., "The Silence Breakers," *Time*, December 6, 2017. https://time.com.

Websites

A Call to Men (www.acalltomen.org). A Call to Men works with males of all ages to promote respectful behaviors and reduce the incidence of sexual harassment and other types of sexual misconduct. The website provides numerous educational materials, as well as a link to the organization's blog, *Out of the Man Box*.

American Civil Liberties Union (ACLU) (www.aclu.org). The ACLU advocates for civil liberties and defends people whose rights are threatened. Its website focuses on issues and rights and provides links to a number of publications about sex discrimination.

Equal Opportunity Employment Commission (EEOC) (www.eeoc.gov). The EEOC enforces federal antidiscrimination laws related to any aspect of employment. Numerous materials are available on its website, and the search engine produces a wealth of information on sex discrimination and related issues.

Girls for Gender Equity (www.ggenyc.org). This organization supports the physical, psychological, social, and economic well-being of females of all ages, with a special focus on girls and women of color. The website offers a good collection of information about sexual harassment and other types of sexual misconduct.

Me Too. (https://metoomvmt.org). This site, which is sponsored by the organization Girls for Gender Equity, offers a wealth of information about the #MeToo movement. It features real-life stories, news articles, statistics, a searchable resource library, and a link to its blog.

Time's Up (www.timesupnow.com). Time's Up focuses on helping victims of sexual harassment with legal assistance and on advocating for stronger laws. The website offers a variety of resources, including articles about sexual harassment, news articles, FAQs, and more.

Peggy J. Parks has written more than 150 educational books on a wide variety of topics for students of all ages. She holds a bachelor's degree from Aquinas College in Grand Rapids, Michigan, where she graduated magna cum laude. Parks lives in Muskegon, Michigan, a town she says inspires her writing because of its location on the shores of beautiful Lake Michigan.